THE GLOW SKY BOOK

BY ILLUMINATIONS®

FEATURING 300 GLOW IN THE DARK STAR DECALS TO ILLUMINATE 24 CONSTELLATIONS! INCLUDES MYTHS, LEGENDS & LORE!

Conceptual Design & Creative Direction - John Bush
Art Direction, Research & Editing - John Childress
Layout & Production Design - Laurel Sullivan
Production Coordination - Lynne Hartwell
Text Research & Writing - Chryste Hall
Paintings - Dawn Scaltreto

ABOUT CONSTELLATIONS AND MYTHOLOGY

Constellations exist only in the minds of human beings. They are projected onto random groups of stars to create a picture story. These pictures have appeared in the sky every year at the same time for thousands of years.

From very early in recorded history, the stars were important to people in their daily lives. The stars assisted the ancients in planning for the planting of their crops, guiding navigators on their many adventures, and as a way of telling time. Much wonder and mystery was associated with the stars, and the people of ancient times began to place a grander, often divine, meaning on the majestic heavenly bodies.

We all are indebted to Greece for the many fascinating myths of the constellations, such as the legends of Andromeda, Orion and Hercules. Astronomy, like a golden chain, runs through history and links together all tribes and peoples of Earth.

The wealth of stars illuminated each evening, and the many constellations in which they are contained, is in fact the oldest historical picture book of all time. Without television, videos, or movies, the sky was the magic light show, continually changing with each season. People would sit outdoors in groups and watch the sky for hours every night as the constellations revealed themselves.

Today, more than eighty constellations and 1,000,000 stars are acknowledged to reside in the sky. Soon astronomers will have identified in excess of 40,000,000 stars. What new constellations will we create, what stories will we tell?

---

*Note To Parents: The classical Greek myths described here are allegories of gods, demi gods and superhumans. The occasional violence associated with these myths may be explained to a child as a super hero story - larger than life.

HOW TO USE THE GLOW SKY BOOK

This is the only book that can be enjoyed in the light or dark! Affix the glow stars to each constellation page and you are ready for the full effect.

Read the story of the constellation, learning about the myths and legends. Enjoy the sky picture of the constellation and how the stars represent it. Now turn out the light and see how it actually appears in the night sky - glowing brightly in the dark.

After you have experienced all the constellations in the dark, and can recognize them, you are ready to find them in the sky. Use the 4 seasons' star maps on the first page of this book to locate them.

When you look into the night sky, remember you are joining a tradition of star gazers tens of thousands of years old. You are the newest generation to discover the brilliant picture book of the glow sky.

HOW TO CREATE YOUR GLOW SKY BOOK:

1. Open the glow stars package on the inside cover and remove the glow in the dark stars sheet.

2. There are three sizes of stars corresponding to the stars printed on each constellation.

3. Peel and stick the stars onto each of the 24 constellations.

4. Now, turn out the lights after reading about the constellation and see the stars glowing as they appear in the sky.

5. Remember, each glow page needs to be exposed to a light source for 30 seconds or more for the maximum brilliance.

6. Enjoy holding the shining heavens in your hands!

STAR CHARTS
The Northern Sky in Fall & Winter

FALL

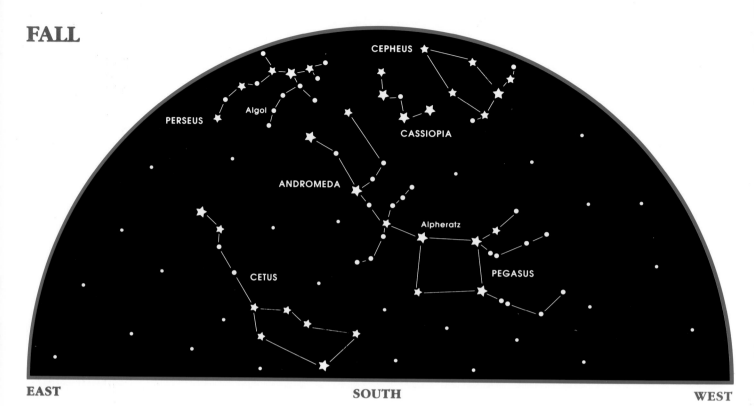

EAST   SOUTH   WEST

View of the night sky looking south in the Fall.

WINTER

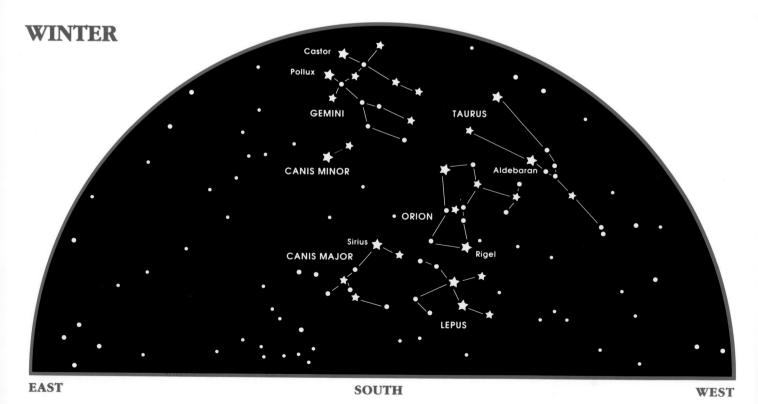

EAST   SOUTH   WEST

View of the night sky looking south in the Winter.

STAR CHARTS
The Northern Sky in Spring & Summer

SPRING

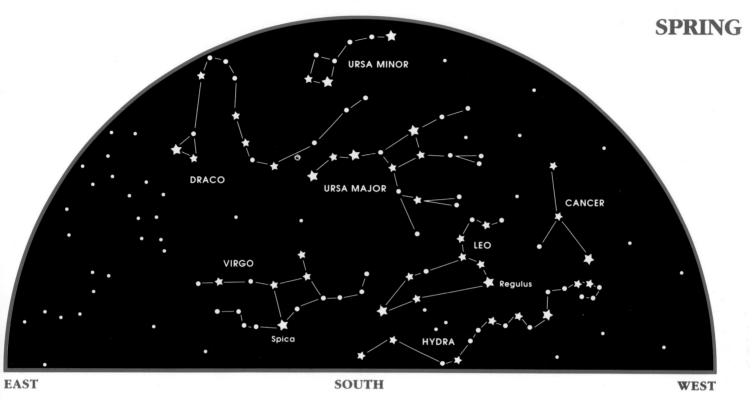

EAST · SOUTH · WEST

View of the night sky looking south in the Spring.

SUMMER

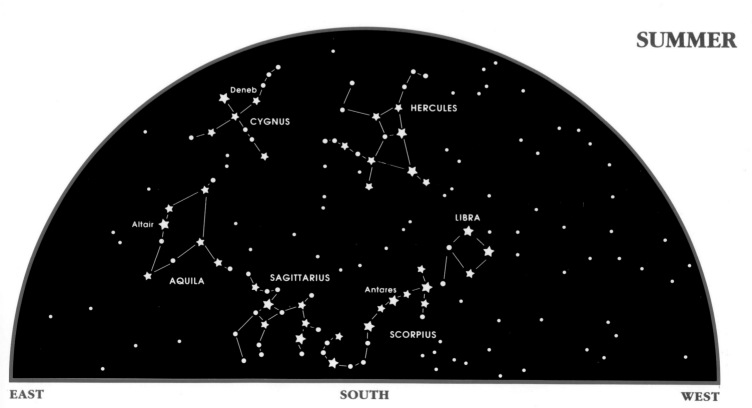

EAST · SOUTH · WEST

View of the night sky looking south in the Summer.

CASSIOPEIA
The Queen

Cassiopeia is one of the best known constellations, located in the far northern sky. When Cassiopeia is located above the pole, she looks like the letter "M". When in the northwestern sky, like the letter "E". When she is located below the pole, much like a "W", and when in the northeastern sky, like the number "3".

Cassiopeia was the legendary queen of Ethiopia, known throughout the land for her elegant beauty. Becoming increasingly vain, Cassiopeia boasted that she was even more lovely than the Sea Nymphs, goddesses of unmatched beauty who ruled over nature. Enraged by Cassiopeia's false bragging, the Sea Nymphs begged the God of the Sea, Poseidon, to punish the queen for her insults and conceit. Poseidon was so angry with Cassiopeia that he unleashed the horrible sea monster Cetus the Whale, and sent him to destroy the coast of Cassiopeia's homeland. The Sea Nymphs also sought eternal punishment for Cassiopeia, arranging for her to be placed in the heavens tied to a chair. In the northern sky Cassiopeia sits, forever circling the celestial pole.

ANDROMEDA
The Chained Maiden

Andromeda can be seen clearly on nights between September and February. It is so close to the Great Square that it shares the star Alpheratz. The Great Square is easily found high in the southern sky. Once you have found Alpheratz, it is easy to locate the stars that form Andromeda's arms, legs and body.

As the frightful sea monster, Cetus, ravaged the Ethiopian coast, Cassiopeia pleaded with Zeus, the all-powerful King of Gods, for his help in driving Cetus from her shores. Zeus ruled that Queen Cassiopeia and King Cepheus must sacrifice their only daughter, Princess Andromeda, to soothe the anger of Poseidon. After much hesitation a tearful Cassiopeia gave up Andromeda, who was chained to a rocky ridge at the edge of the sea so that Cetus may come and devour her. As Andromeda awaited her sorrowful fate, the brave champion Perseus miraculously appeared and disposed of the sea monster for all time. Perseus then released Andromeda, and the princess sailed away with the hero to become his bride. The two went on to live a long and happy life together.

CEPHEUS
The King

Cepheus, a well known constellation for thousands of years, resembles the shape a child might draw of a house with a steep roof. The easiest way to find Cepheus is to locate the north star, nearby you will easily find the top of the "roof".

King Cepheus was the husband of Queen Cassiopeia and the father of the lovely Princess Andromeda. Upon his death, Cepheus was placed in the heavens to spend eternity with his beloved wife and daughter. He is included among the group of constellations known as The Royal Family in the Sky, which also contains Cassiopeia, Andromeda and Perseus as well as Cetus and the winged horse Pegasus. Cepheus is the dimmest of these constellations. This is probably because of the small part he played in the events caused by Cassiopeia's vanity. The Royal Family of the Sky is perhaps the best example of how the constellations are arranged so that their individual stories, when connected, portray a complete history, and are remembered for all time.

CETUS
The Sea Monster

Cetus is one of the earliest constellations named by man and is the fourth largest in the sky. Occupying a huge region of the southern sky, it is exceeded in area only by the constellations Ursa Major, Virgo and Hydra.

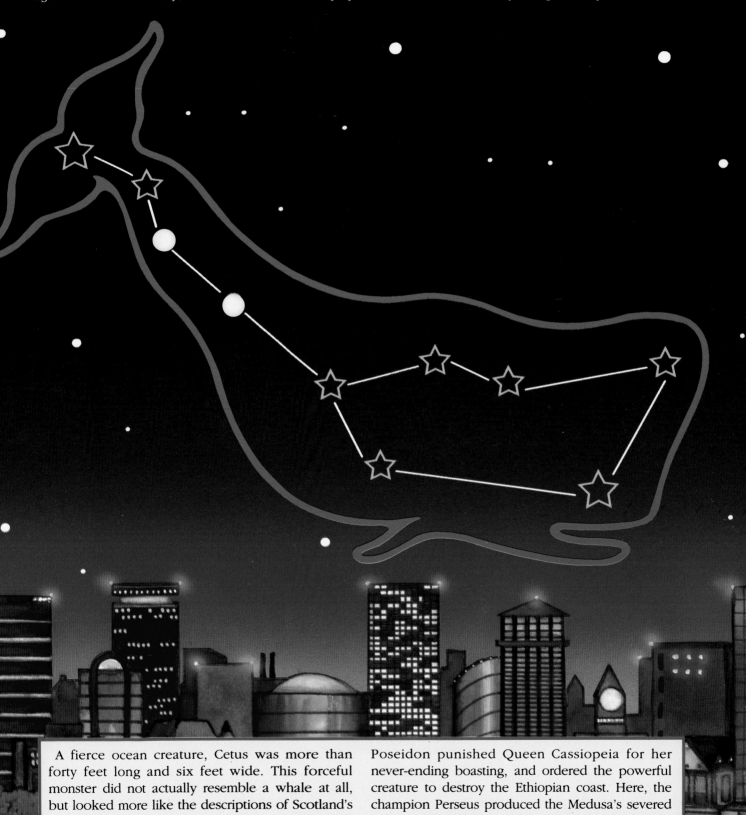

A fierce ocean creature, Cetus was more than forty feet long and six feet wide. This forceful monster did not actually resemble a whale at all, but looked more like the descriptions of Scotland's Loch Ness monster. Poseidon is said to have created Cetus as a representation of the power of the deep sea, and sent the sea monster on many missions of destruction. Cetus met his death when Poseidon punished Queen Cassiopeia for her never-ending boasting, and ordered the powerful creature to destroy the Ethiopian coast. Here, the champion Perseus produced the Medusa's severed head, whose fatal gaze instantly turned Cetus to stone. Because of his faithful service, Cetus was given a place among the stars in the region known as The Sea, where ocean creatures abound.

PERSEUS
The Champion

The constellation Perseus is located along the Milky Way and is the point in the sky from which the Perseid meteor showers seem to originate. The meteor showers always occur around August 12th every year and average about 50 meteors every hour.

Perseus was the son of Zeus and Danea, princess of Argos. His most dangerous quest was to kill the Gorgon Medusa, one of three hideous creatures with body scales, wings and a tangle of snakes for hair. To catch a glimpse of a Gorgon turned one at once to stone. As Perseus was a favorite of the gods, he received their valuable assistance to accomplish his mission. From Athena, Goddess of Defensive War, he accepted a shiny bronze shield which he used as a mirror to avoid the Gorgon's gaze. By Hermes, the God of Travelers, he was given an unbreakable sword which he used to cut off Medusa's head. His expedition was so successful that Perseus gained everlasting fame. At his death he was transported to the starry skies, where he resides beside his precious wife, Andromeda.

PEGASUS
The Winged Horse

Pegasus is created by fourteen stars that seem to form the shape of half a horse. It is easier to find this constellation by looking for a group of four stars called the Great Square. Look high to the south skies to locate the Great Square. To the right of the square sits Pegasus. September through January is the ideal viewing time.

ALPHERATZ

A snow white, winged horse with a mane of glittering gold, Pegasus was the son of Poseidon and the Gorgon Medusa. As Perseus beheaded Medusa, Pegasus was born from its blood which fell into the sea, creating a frothing foam. One fated day, Athena gave Pegasus to the warrior Bellerophon to aid him in defeating the Chimaera, a dreadful monster which was part lion, part serpent and part goat. Bellerophon was so proud after his successful conquest that he boldly attempted to ride Pegasus to Mount Olympus, home of the Gods where mortals do not dwell. Zeus became infuriated at Bellerophon's self importance and caused the flying horse to throw his rider. Alone, Pegasus soared to the heavens where he became the Thundering Horse of Zeus and carrier of the divine lightning.

ORION
The Great Hunter

The best time to view Orion is from December through March. It is one of the easiest constellations to find, and is the brightest constellation in the winter sky. Find the position of Orion on the charts. Look to the south as you picture its shape. The three stars you see lined up in the middle of the constellation are called Orion's Belt.

ORION'S BELT

To reward King Hyrieus for his gracious hospitality, Zeus, Poseidon and Hermes presented him with a magnificent son, Orion. The most beautiful man the world had ever known, Prince Orion was an enormous giant, who grew to such height that he was able to walk on the floor of the sea without wetting his head. Orion became a strong and skillful hunter, easily defeating the most savage of beasts. As his hunting skills became more powerful, Orion boasted that no animal on earth could escape him. Angered by Orion's boasting, the gods sent a poisonous scorpion to defeat Orion, sending the able hunter to his end. At the request of Artemis, Goddess of the Hunt, Orion was honorably placed among the stars. Adorned in shiny, golden armor, The Hunter forever stands.

CANIS MAJOR & MINOR
The Greater and Lesser Dogs

Canis Major and Canis MInor are said to be Orion's legendary hunting dogs. One easy way to locate Canis Major is to imagine drawing a line pointing southeastward through the three bright stars that form Orion's belt. To locate Canis Minor, imagine a line drawn eastward through Orion's shoulders.

Always following the legendary Orion on his exciting adventures, Canis Major and Canis Minor were two of the giant's loyal hunting dogs. The Greater Dog, Canis Major, stands in the sky on his hind feet watching his master, or springing after The Hare, Lepus, which closely hides under Orion's feet. The wide stretched jaws of Canis Major sparkle with the brightest of all fixed stars, Sirius, which signifies brightness and heat. Canis Minor, The Lesser Dog, a well trained house or watch dog which accompanied Orion on his hunting trips, owes its fame in the heavens to the first magnitude star, Procyon. The expression "Dog Days of Summer" came into being because the rising of the stars Procyon and Sirius often corresponded with periods of extreme heat.

LEPUS
The Hare

Lepus, another popular ancient constellation, is said to have been the favorite hunting prey of Orion. Lepus, small and faint in the sky, can be found hiding below Orion's feet, and to the west of Sirius, the brilliant star of Canis Major.

Lepus, the Hare, was one of the animals that the great hunter Orion most delighted in pursuing. Lepus was thus honored with a place among the stars. Crouching low on the horizon, The Hare tries to remain unnoticed as it endlessly attempts to escape Orion's attention and attack. Through the legend of Lepus, the timid hare is seen fleeing before Orion as The Hunter is poised to attack the onrushing bull, Taurus. Meanwhile, the fierce monster of the deep, Cetus the Whale, eagerly seeks any prey that he may savagely devour, and The Champion, Perseus, with drawn sword, stands ever ready to join in mortal combat. For all time, the myths and legends of ancient life shall be remembered through the many amazing tales illuminated by the constellations.

TAURUS
The Bull

To find Taurus in the southern sky, first look at your star chart for its position and imagine the shape as you look into the sky. Taurus is a large, but fairly faint constellation which adjoins Orion.

ALDEBARAN

The delightful daughter of Agenor, Europa, was so beautiful that Zeus immediately fell in love with her. Determined to win Europa's heart, Zeus assumed the form of a milky white bull, whose horns were crowned with flowers, and mingled with the herds of Agenor. Europa was enchanted with the sight of this splendid creature, and climbed upon its back. Taking advantage of his good fortune, Zeus carried the fair maiden away from her homeland, across the seas to the island of Crete. Here, Europa gave birth to Minos, father of the creature Minotaur, who was half bull and half man. Zeus celebrated his love for Europa by having the continent Europe named after her, and created the constellation Taurus, to be seen in the sky for eternity, the symbol of fertility and power.

GEMINI
The Twins

Gemini, one of the most popular and brilliant constellations in the night sky, is one of the few marked by bright stars. Easily found on nights between December and March, look for the two bright stars Castor and Pollux. The lines of the fainter stars extending from the two form the bodies of the twins.

After Zeus, disguised as a graceful swan, visited Queen Leda of Sparta, she gave birth to twin sons, Castor and Pollux. The two boys were devoted and loving brothers who later became as different in nature as they appeared alike as twins. The mortal Castor developed into a master horseman, while the immortal Pollux became a famous boxer. Together, The Twins grew to become skillful war- riors. When Castor was killed in battle, Pollux, who was so very attached to his brother, could not bear to continue on without him. Stricken with great sorrow, Pollux asked of their father, Zeus, to bring Castor back to life. Zeus, touched by this dis- play of devoted brotherly love, arranged for The Twins to stay endlessly side by, side among the stars as the brilliant constellation Gemini.

URSA MAJOR & MINOR
The Greater and Lesser Bears

Ursa Major and Ursa Minor contains two of the most visible star groups in the sky, the Big Dipper and the Little Dipper. They are both easily seen year round on any clear night. Find the positions of both star groups on your charts and picture their shapes as you face south and look into the sky.

THE LITTLE DIPPER

THE BIG DIPPER

Castillo was the splendid Princess of Arcadia who captured Zeus' heart, and gave birth to his son, Arcas. Seething with jealousy, the Queen of the Gods, Hera, unleashed her mighty wrath and transformed Castillo into a bear, doomed to prowl the forests forever. Years later, while Arcas was out hunting, the vengeful Hera brought Castillo before the young man as prey. While Arcas unknowingly prepared to kill his mother, Zeus swiftly stepped between them and sent Castillo soaring into the heavens to become Ursa Major, The Greater Bear. Later, the King of the Gods placed Arcas in the sky to be forever known as Ursa Minor, The Lesser Bear, reuniting mother and son for all time. Ursa Major, also called the Big Dipper, is the best known constellation in the northern sky.

VIRGO
The Virgin

You can find Virgo sitting high in the southern sky. To the right of Virgo you will find the star Denebola, which also makes up the tail of Leo. The most visible star in this group is called Spica, which means, "spike of grain". Virgo is easily seen on nights in April and June.

SPICA

References to the constellation of Virgo, The Virgin, are found in astronomical records of every age and race, suggesting that this was one of the first star groups to receive a name. In Greek mythology, The Virgin is considered to be Demeter, the Goddess of the Harvest, as well as her daughter, Persephone, who winters in the underworld and then returns to the earth with the dawn of spring.

On ancient maps, The Virgin is depicted as a robust woman with wings, who is forever walking. In her left hand she carries a symbol of the harvest, a head of wheat or perhaps an ear of corn, marked by the brilliant star, Spica. Placed in the heavens by the gods to characterize the harvest season and the images of springtime, The Virgin is to remind us of nature and wholeness.

DRACO
The Dragon

The long, winding star pattern of Draco is remarkably dragon-like as it snakes its way around the sky toward Cepheus. In most northern latitudes, Draco never sets below the horizon, due to its location high in the north sky. Draco is the eighth largest constellation in the night sky.

Known for its sharp vision and vigilance, Draco, The Dragon was the traditional guardian of temples and treasures as well as the springs of life and immortality. Hera, Queen of the Gods, enlisted the assistance of Draco to serve as protector of the precious golden apples, which she had presented to Zeus on the day of their wedding. While performing this task, Draco was tragically slain by The Hero, Hercules, who stole away with the golden apples, which became a symbol of his immortality. Outraged by Hercules' daring accomplishment, Queen Hera rewarded Draco for his faithfulness by lifting him up into the sky to be remembered forever as a constellation and to be seen by all for eternity. Today the Dragon peacefully winds and twists around the North Celestial Pole.

HYDRA
The Water Snake

Hydra is the largest and longest constellation, sprawling eastward a quarter of the way around the sky. You can locate the head of Hydra by looking south of Cancer and East of Canis MInor. Hydra is so huge that it takes more than six hours for the whole constellation to rise in the sky.

Hydra was a monstrous water snake who lived in the marshes of Lerna, often attacking the people of the nearby country of Argos. This fierce serpent had nine heads, the center head being immortal. As one of the twelve labors ordered by Zeus, Hercules was sent to destroy the many-headed monster. This task appeared impossible, as each time one of the monster's heads was severed, two new ones grew in its place. Much discouraged, Hercules sought the advice of his clever nephew, Iolaus, who suggested burning off the heads of the serpent. The two successfully accomplished this, finally burying the central, indestructible head of Hydra. The victorious Hercules then dipped his arrows in Hydra's immortal blood, forever rendering the wounds he inflicted deadly.

CANCER
The Crab

Cancer, one of the best known constellations, has no bright stars to mark it. It can only be seen with the unaided eye on very dark, clear nights. To find Cancer, look for the sickle of Leo, just to the east, and the bright pair of Gemini, Castor and Pollux just to the west.

As Hercules struggled to defeat the hideous nine-headed Hydra, Queen Hera, his immortal enemy, ordered Cancer, The Crab to go and harass The Hero. The Crab snapped at Hercules' ankles as he bravely fought with Hydra. Unbothered by Cancers' efforts, The Hero easily crushed the crab to pieces under the heel of his foot and went on to successfully destroy the monstrous snake. In gratitude for The Crab's courageous attempt to fulfill her angry wrath, Hera gifted Cancer with a place among the stars as a constellation. Located between Gemini and Leo, The Crab remains eternally perched just above Hydra, which is the longest constellation, eagerly awaiting an opportunity to seize the monster in its vise-like claws.

Leo's best viewing time is from February to June. You can find Leo by facing south and looking high into the southern sky. It is easy to find because it includes a star group known as the Sickle, which looks like a backward question mark and forms the lion's head.

Sickle

REGULUS

The fist labor imposed on The Hero, Hercules, by almighty Zeus was to slay Leo, the frightful lion which roamed the forest of Nemaea. Hercules accomplished this task with the utmost of ease, simply strangling the fierce beast with his bare hands. From this point on, the courageous hero wore the lion's skin over his shoulders, assuring him eternal protection from harm. In memory of this dreadful battle, Zeus placed the proud and passionate lion in the heavens to eternally symbolize the challenges of kingship. The constellation of Leo contains the enormously bright star, Regulus, known as "the star of the king," perhaps referring to Alexander the Great, King of Macedonia who, during his lifetime, ruled the entire known world, was born during the Lion month.

HERCULES
The Hero

Hercules, the fifth largest of the constellations, appears fairly dim in the night sky. Hercules is depicted as a kneeling man with one foot on the head of Draco, however it takes quite a bit of imagination to see any resemblance to a man in this star group. Seen below, Hercules is in an upright position, but in the sky he appears upside down.

The strongest man ever to walk the earth, Hercules was the son of Zeus and the fair maiden Alcmene of Thebes. Maddened by Zeus' constant affairs, Hera concentrated her vicious anger upon the mighty hero Hercules. When he was grown, and a happily married man, Hera sought her final revenge by causing him to lose control of his senses. She then led the unsuspecting hero to believe that his much-loved family was a pack of wild animals, and in his confusion he killed them. Zeus, outraged by this disaster, ordered Hercules to undertake twelve difficult labors as punishment for his horrible sin. Completing this mission, Hercules managed to save his soul, and was welcomed into the heavens with a blinding flash of lightning which radiated from the sky.

While Cronus, father of Zeus, was courting the mortal woman Philyra he assumed the form of a stallion to avoid the fury of his jealous wife, Rhea. From this union was born Chiron, the most famous of centaurs and a skillful archer. Although centaurs, creatures who are part man and part horse, were generally savage and cruel, Chiron was wise, gentle and good. As the teacher of several famous heroes, he educated the boys about the mysteries of life. One fated day, Chiron was mistakenly slain by his student, Hercules. Realizing the wound was incurable, Chiron begged Zeus to deprive him of immortality. Pitying his half-brother's predicament, Zeus granted the request and located Chiron in the sky as the constellation Sagittarius, where The Archer stands with bow and arrow for all time.

CYGNUS
The Swan

Cygnus is one of the very few constellations that actually looks like what it is supposed to represent. To find Cygnus is a little trickier than that for most constellations. Face north and look over your right shoulder for the very bright star, Vega. Beneath Vega, find the row of stars forming the swan's neck. From there it is easy to see the shape of its tail and wings.

DENEB

 Just as he was beginning his life as a great Trojan hero, Cygnus was tragicaly killed in battle by the famed and clever warrior, Achilles. As Cygnus drew a last breath of life, his father, Poseidon, transformed the young man into a beautiful swan and carried him to the heights of Mount Olympus, home of the gods. Here, Cygnus displayed his grand grace and elegance, inspiring the King of the Gods to change himself into a swan. Disguised as the majestic creature, Zeus sped to earth and courted the lovely Leda, who gave birth to their twin sons, Castor and Pollux. Zeus also took the form of the swan to trick Nemesis, the stern goddess of Divinity, from Cygnus' attack. In the starry skies, the great white swan forever flies, with wings outstretched, southward along the Milky Way.

AQUILA
The Eagle

Aquila lies along the summer Milky Way, an excellent area to explore with binoculars. To locate Aquila the Eagle, look for the star Altair. Altair is the center and brightest star of a line of three stars. This almost straight line of stars represent the eagles wings.

ALTAIR

Aquila, The Eagle, was the divine bird of Zeus and bearer of his sacred thunder. Aquila began serviceing the King of the Gods as Zeus was battling with his father, Cronus, to gain control of the universe. During this fierce combat Aquila faithfully provided his master with plentiful food, drink and weapons, enabling Zeus to become victorious in his quest for supreme power. Aquila continued to faithfully attend to his lord's wants and needs, and when Zeus enlisted the young Trojan boy, Ganymede, the powerful eagle descended to gather him. Aquila then carried Ganymede through the air to Mount Olympus, where he became the cupbearer of the gods. Zeus was so pleased with Aquila's actions that he placed The Eagle among the stars to eternally soar through the sky.

SCORPIUS
The Scorpion

Scorpius is a southern constellation, relatively small, but brilliant, and the envy of northern astronomers. To find Scorpius look for an arc of four stars in the southern sky that form its "head". To the left of the head is the large red star Antares. Below Antares look for the string of stars that form the scorpions tail. Best viewing time is from July through August.

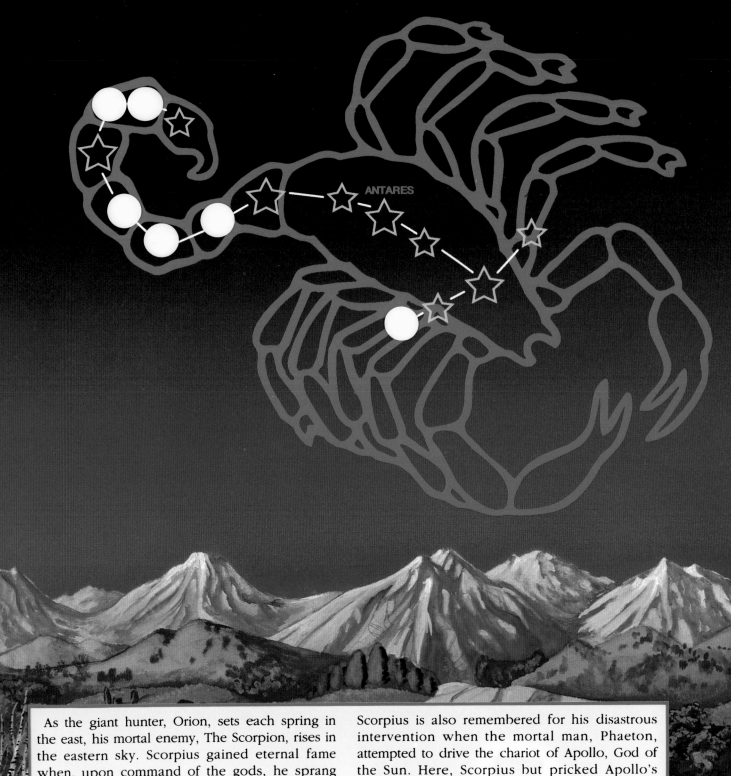

ANTARES

As the giant hunter, Orion, sets each spring in the east, his mortal enemy, The Scorpion, rises in the eastern sky. Scorpius gained eternal fame when, upon command of the gods, he sprang from the earth to surprise Orion, and sent the able hunter to his final resting place. Even the God of Healing, Asclepius, was unable to reverse the fatal effects of The Scorpion's sharp sting.

Scorpius is also remembered for his disastrous intervention when the mortal man, Phaeton, attempted to drive the chariot of Apollo, God of the Sun. Here, Scorpius but pricked Apollo's horses with his lethal sting, causing the creatures to bolt and driving the sun-bearing chariot recklessly through the heavens, drying up many rivers and scorching the earth below.

Libra is a faint constellation, one of many without any bright stars. In ancient times the stars of Libra formed the claws of Scorpius, the Scorpion.

During the Golden Age, the legendary first period of human existence, Astraea, the Roman Goddess of Justice, lived on the earth, mingling among the many mortal beings. In the pans of her great golden scales, she heavily weighed the good and evil deeds of men and women, thereby deciding their many different fates. As Astraea became increasingly offended by the wickedness of her citizens, she decided to flee from the corrupt civilization, and returned to the heavens, joining Demeter as the constellation of the Virgin Goddess. Astraea abandoned civilization so hurredly that she left behind her golden scales of justice. The Romans, in fear of her judgement, created the constellation of Libra from the ancient Scorpion's claws so that The Scales would always be nearby in the sky.